CARYL CHURCHILL

Caryl Churchill has written fo............................radio.
Her stage plays include *Owners* (Royal Court Theatre Upstairs, 1972); *Objections to Sex and Violence* (Royal Court, 1975); *Light Shining in Buckinghamshire* (Joint Stock on tour incl. Theatre Upstairs, 1976); *Vinegar Tom* (Monstrous Regiment on tour, incl. Half Moon and ICA, 1976); *Traps* (Theatre Upstairs, 1977), *Cloud Nine* (Joint Stock on tour incl. Royal Court, London, 1979, then Theatre de Lys, New York, 1981); *Three More Sleepless Nights* (Soho Poly and Theatre Upstairs, 1980); *Top Girls* (Royal Court, London, then Public Theatre, New York, 1982); *Fen* (Joint Stock on tour, incl. Almeida and Royal Court, London, then Public Theatre, New York, 1983); *Softcops* (RSC at the Pit, 1984); *A Mouthful of Birds* with David Lan (Joint Stock on tour, incl. Royal Court, 1986); *Serious Money* (Royal Court and Wyndham's, London, then Public Theatre, New York, 1987); *Icecream* (Royal Court, 1989); *Mad Forest* (Central School of Speech and Drama, then Royal Court, 1990); *Lives of the Great Poisoners* with Orlando Gough and Ian Spink (Second Stride on tour, incl. Riverside Studios, London, 1991); *The Skriker* (Royal National Theatre, 1994); *Thyestes* translated from Seneca (Royal Court Theatre Upstairs, 1994); *Hotel* with Orlando Gough and Ian Spink (Second Stride on tour, incl. The Place, London, 1997); *This is a Chair* (London International Festival of Theatre at the Royal Court, 1997); *Blue Heart* (Joint Stock on tour, incl. Royal Court Theatre, 1997); *Far Away* (Royal Court Theatre Upstairs and Albery Theatre, London, 2000/01; New York Theatre Workshop 2002); *A Number* (Royal Court Theatre, 2002).

Other works by this author in the same series

CARYL CHURCHILL

Far Away

NICK HERN BOOKS

London

www.nickhernbooks.co.uk

A Nick Hern Book

Far Away first published in 2000 as a paperback original
by Nick Hern Books, 14 Larden Road, London W3 7ST
in association with the Royal Court Theatre

Reprinted 2003

Far Away copyright © 2000 by Caryl Churchill Ltd

Caryl Churchill has asserted her right to be identified
as the author of this work

Cover: Ned Hoste, 2H

Typeset by Country Setting, Kingsdown, Kent, CT14 8ES
Printed and bound in Great Britain by Biddles of Guildford

ISBN 1-85459-744-2

Far Away was first performed at the Royal Court Theatre Upstairs, London, on 24 November 2000, before transferring to the Albery Theatre in the West End on 18 January 2001. The cast was as follows:

YOUNG JOAN	Annabelle Seymour-Julen
HARPER	Linda Bassett
TODD	Kevin McKidd
OLDER JOAN	Katherine Tozer

Director   Stephen Daldry
Designer   Ian MacNeil
Lighting Designer   Rick Fisher
Sound Designer   Paul Arditti

FAR AWAY

Characters

JOAN, *a girl*

HARPER, *her aunt*

TODD, *a young man*

The Parade (Scene 2.5): five is too few and twenty better than ten. A hundred?

1.

HARPER*'s house. Night.*

JOAN   I can't sleep.

HARPER   It's the strange bed.

JOAN   No, I like different places.

HARPER   Are you cold?

JOAN   No.

HARPER   Do you want a drink?

JOAN   I think I am cold.

HARPER   That's easy enough then. There's extra
            blankets in the cupboard.

JOAN   Is it late?

HARPER   Two.

JOAN   Are you going to bed?

HARPER   Do you want a hot drink?

JOAN   No thank you.

HARPER   I should go to bed then.

JOAN   Yes.

HARPER   It's always odd in a new place. When you've been here a week you'll look back at tonight and it won't seem the same at all.

JOAN   I've been to a lot of places. I've stayed with friends at their houses. I don't miss my parents if you think that.

HARPER   Do you miss your dog?

JOAN   I miss the cat I think.

HARPER   Does it sleep on your bed?

JOAN   No because I chase it off. But it gets in if the door's not properly shut. You think you've shut the door but it hasn't caught and she pushes it open in the night.

HARPER   Come here a minute. You're shivering. Are you hot?

JOAN   No, I'm all right.

HARPER   You're over-tired. Go to bed. I'm going to bed myself.

JOAN   I went out.

HARPER   When? just now?

JOAN   Just now.

HARPER   No wonder you're cold. It's hot in the
            daytime here but it's cold at night.

JOAN   The stars are brighter here than at
            home.

HARPER   It's because there's no street lights.

JOAN   I couldn't see much.

HARPER   I don't expect you could. How did you
            get out? I didn't hear the door.

JOAN   I went out the window.

HARPER   I'm not sure I like that.

JOAN   No it's quite safe, there's a roof and a
            tree.

HARPER   When people go to bed they should
            stay in bed. Do you climb out of the
            window at home?

JOAN   I can't at home because - No I don't.

HARPER   I'm responsible for you.

JOAN   Yes, I'm sorry.

HARPER   Well that's enough adventures for one
            night. You'll sleep now. Off you go.
            Look at you, you're asleep on your feet.

JOAN   There was a reason.

HARPER   For going out?

JOAN   I heard a noise.

HARPER   An owl?

JOAN   A shriek.

HARPER   An owl then. There are all sorts of
            birds here, you might see a golden
            oriole. People come here specially to
            watch birds and we sometimes make
            tea or coffee or sell bottles of water
            because there's no café and people
            don't expect that and they get thirsty.
            You'll see in the morning what a
            beautiful place it is.

JOAN   It was more like a person screaming.

HARPER   It is like a person screaming when you
            hear an owl.

JOAN   It was a person screaming.

HARPER   Poor girl, what a fright you must have had imagining you heard somebody screaming. You should have come straight down here to me.

JOAN   I wanted to see.

HARPER   It was dark.

JOAN   Yes but I did see.

HARPER   Now what did you imagine you saw in the dark?

JOAN   I saw my uncle.

HARPER   Yes I expect you did. He likes a breath of air. He wasn't screaming I hope?

JOAN   No.

HARPER   That's all right then. Did you talk to him? I expect you were frightened he'd say what are you doing out of your bed so late.

JOAN   I stayed in the tree.

HARPER   He didn't see you?

JOAN   No.

HARPER   He'll be surprised won't he, he'll laugh when he hears you were up in the tree. He'll be cross but he doesn't mean it,

he'll think it's a good joke, it's the sort
of thing he did when he was a boy. So
bed now. I'll go up too.

JOAN   He was pushing someone. He was
bundling someone into a shed.

HARPER   He must have been putting a big sack
in the shed. He works too late.

JOAN   I'm not sure if it was a woman. It
could have been a young man.

HARPER   Well I have to tell you, when you've
been married as long as I have. There
are things people get up to, it's natural,
it's nothing bad, that's just friends of his
your uncle was having a little party
with.

JOAN   Was it a party?

HARPER   Just a little party.

JOAN   Yes because there wasn't just that one
person.

HARPER   No, there'd be a few of his friends.

JOAN   There was a lorry.

HARPER   Yes, I expect there was.

JOAN   When I put my ear against the side of the lorry I heard crying inside.

HARPER   How could you do that from up in the tree?

JOAN   I got down from the tree. I went to the lorry after I looked in the window of the shed.

HARPER   There might be things that are not your business when you're a visitor in someone else's house.

JOAN   Yes, I'd rather not have seen. I'm sorry.

HARPER   Nobody saw you?

JOAN   They were thinking about themselves.

HARPER   I think it's lucky nobody saw you.

JOAN   If it's a party, why was there so much blood?

HARPER   There isn't any blood.

JOAN   Yes.

HARPER   Where?

JOAN   On the ground.

HARPER   In the dark? how would you see that in
                the dark?

JOAN   I slipped in it.

                She holds up her bare foot.

                I mostly wiped it off.

HARPER   That's where the dog got run over this
                afternoon.

JOAN   Wouldn't it have dried up?

HARPER   Not if the ground was muddy.

JOAN   What sort of dog?

HARPER   A big dog, a big mongrel.

JOAN   That's awful, you must be very sad, had
                you had him long?

HARPER   No, he was young, he ran out, he was
                never very obedient, a lorry was
                backing up.

JOAN   What was his name?

HARPER   Flash.

JOAN   What colour was he?

HARPER   Black with a bit of white.

JOAN   Why were the children in the shed?

HARPER   What children?

JOAN   Don't you know what children?

HARPER   How could you see there were
            children?

JOAN   There was a light on. That's how I
            could see the blood inside the shed. I
            could see the faces and which ones had
            blood on.

HARPER   You've found out something secret. You
            know that don't you?

JOAN   Yes.

HARPER   Something you shouldn't know.

JOAN   Yes I'm sorry.

HARPER   Something you must never talk about.
            Because if you do you could put
            people's lives in danger.

JOAN   Why? who from? from my uncle?

HARPER   Of course not from your uncle.

JOAN   From you?

HARPER   Of course not from me, are you mad?
          I'm going to tell you what's going on.
          Your uncle is helping these people. He's
          helping them escape. He's giving them
          shelter. Some of them were still in the
          lorry, that's why they were crying. Your
          uncle's going to take them all into the
          shed and then they'll be all right.

JOAN   They had blood on their faces.

HARPER   That's from before. That's because they
          were attacked by the people your
          uncle's saving them from.

JOAN   There was blood on the ground.

HARPER   One of them was injured very badly
          but your uncle bandaged him up.

JOAN   He's helping them.

HARPER   That's right.

JOAN   There wasn't a dog. There wasn't a
          party.

HARPER   No, I'm trusting you with the truth
          now. You must never talk about it or
          you'll put your uncle's life in danger
          and mine and even your own. You
          won't even say anything to your parents.

JOAN   Why did you have me to stay if you've
        got this secret going on?

HARPER The lorry should have come yesterday.
        It won't happen again while you're
        here.

JOAN   It can now because I know. You don't
        have to stop for me. I could help uncle
        in the shed and look after them.

HARPER No, he has to do it himself. But thank
        you for offering, that's very kind. So
        after all that excitement do you think
        you could go back to bed?

JOAN   Why was uncle hitting them?

HARPER Hitting who?

JOAN   He was hitting a man with a stick. I
        think the stick was metal. He hit one of
        the children.

HARPER One of the people in the lorry was a
        traitor. He wasn't really one of them,
        he was pretending, he was going to
        betray them, they found out and told
        your uncle. Then he attacked your
        uncle, he attacked the other people,
        your uncle had to fight him.

JOAN   That's why there was so much blood.

HARPER   Yes, it had to be done to save the
              others.

JOAN   He hit one of the children.

HARPER   That would have been the child of the
              traitor. Or sometimes you get bad
              children who even betray their parents.

JOAN   What's going to happen?

HARPER   They'll go off in the lorry very early in
              the morning.

JOAN   Where to?

HARPER   Where they're escaping to. You don't
              want to have to keep any more secrets.

JOAN   He only hit the traitors.

HARPER   Of course. I'm not surprised you can't
              sleep, what an upsetting thing to see.
              But now you understand, it's not so
              bad. You're part of a big movement
              now to make things better. You can be
              proud of that. You can look at the stars
              and think here we are in our little bit
              of space, and I'm on the side of the
              people who are putting things right,

and your soul will expand right into the sky.

JOAN   Can't I help?

HARPER   You can help me clean up in the morning. Will you do that?

JOAN   Yes.

HARPER   So you'd better get some sleep.

2.

Several years later. A hat makers.

1.

JOAN *and* TODD *are sitting at a workbench. They have each just started making a hat.*

TODD   There's plenty of blue.

JOAN   I think I'm starting with black.

TODD   Colour always wins.

JOAN   I will have colour, I'm starting with black to set the colour off.

TODD   I did one last week that was an abstract picture of the street, blue for the buses, yellow for the flats, red for the leaves, grey for the sky. Nobody got it but I knew what it was. There's little satisfactions to be had.

JOAN   Don't you enjoy it?

TODD   You're new aren't you?

JOAN   This is my first hat. My first
                professional hat.

TODD   Did you do hat at college?

JOAN   My degree hat was a giraffe six feet
                tall.

TODD   You won't have time to do something
                like that in the week.

JOAN   I know.

TODD   We used to get two weeks before a
                parade and then they took it down to
                one and now they're talking about
                cutting a day.

JOAN   So we'd get an extra day off?

TODD   We'd get a day's less money. We
                wouldn't make such good hats.

JOAN   Can they do that?

TODD   You'd oppose it would you?

JOAN   I've only just started.

TODD   You'll find there's a lot wrong with this
                place.

JOAN   I thought it was one of the best jobs.

TODD   It is. Do you know where to go for
          lunch?

JOAN   I think there's a canteen isn't there?

TODD   Yes but we don't go there. I'll show you
          where to go.

2.

Next day. They are working on the hats, which are by now far
more brightly decorated ie the ones they were working on have
been replaced by ones nearer completion.

JOAN   Your turn.

TODD   I go for a swim in the river before
          work.

JOAN   Isn't it dangerous?

TODD   Your turn.

JOAN   I've got a pilot's licence.

TODD   I stay up till four every morning
          watching the trials.

JOAN   I'm getting a room in a subway.

TODD   I've got my own place.

JOAN   Have you?

TODD   Do you want to see it? That's coming
            on.

JOAN   I don't understand yours but I like the
            feather.

TODD   I'm not trying. I've been here too long.

JOAN   Will you leave?

TODD   My turn. There's something wrong with
            how we get the contracts.

JOAN   But we want the contracts.

TODD   What if we don't deserve them? What
            if our work isn't really the best?

JOAN   So what's going on?

TODD   I'll just say a certain person's brother-
            in-law. Where does he work do you
            think?

JOAN   Where does he work?

TODD   I'm not talking about it in here. Tell
            me something else.

JOAN   I don't like staying in in the evenings
              and watching trials.

TODD   I watch them at night after I come
              back.

JOAN   Back from where?

TODD   Where do you like?

3.

Next day. They're working on the hats, which are getting very big and extravagant.

TODD   I don't enjoy animal hats myself.

JOAN   I was a student.

TODD   Abstract hats are back in a big way.

JOAN   I've always liked abstract hats.

TODD   You must have not noticed when
              everyone hated them.

JOAN   It was probably before my time.

              Silence. They go on working.

JOAN   It's just if you're going on about it all
              the time I don't know why you don't
              do something about it.

TODD   This is your third day.

JOAN   The management's corrupt – you've
              told me. We're too low paid – you've
              told me.

              Silence. They go on working.

TODD   Too much green.

JOAN   It's meant to be too much.

              Silence. They go on working.

TODD   I noticed you looking at that fair boy's
              hat. I hope you told him it was
              derivative.

              Silence. They go on working.

TODD   I'm the only person in this place who's
              got any principles, don't tell me I
              should do something, I spend my days
              wondering what to do.

JOAN   So you'll probably come up with
              something.

              Silence. They go on working.

4.

*Next day. They are working on the hats, which are now
enormous and preposterous.*

TODD   That's beautiful.

JOAN   You like it?

TODD   I do.

JOAN   I like yours too.

TODD   You don't have to say that. It's not one
              of my best.

JOAN   No it's got - I don't know, it's a
              confident hat.

TODD   I have been doing parades for six years.
              So I'm a valued old hand. So when I
              go and speak to a certain person he
              might pay attention.

JOAN   You're going to speak to him?

TODD   I've an appointment after work.

JOAN   You might lose your job.

TODD   I might.

JOAN   I'm impressed.

TODD   That was the idea.

JOAN   Will you mention the brother-in-law?

TODD   First I'll talk about the money. Then I'll
              just touch in the brother-in-law. I've a
              friend who's a journalist.

JOAN   Will you touch in the journalist?

TODD   I might imply something without giving
              the journalist away. It might be better if
              he can't trace the journalist back to me.

JOAN   Though he will suspect.

TODD   However much he suspects. One thing
              if I lost my job.

JOAN   What's that?

TODD   I'd miss you.

JOAN   Already?

5.

Next day. A procession of ragged, beaten, chained prisoners, each wearing a hat, on their way to execution. The finished hats are even more enormous and preposterous than in the previous scene.

6.

A new week. JOAN *and* TODD *are starting work on new hats.*

JOAN   I still can't believe it.

TODD   No one's ever won in their first week before.

JOAN   It's all going to be downhill from now on.

TODD   You can't win every week.

JOAN   That's what I mean.

TODD   No but you'll do a fantastic body of
            work while you're here.

JOAN   Sometimes I think it's a pity that more
            aren't kept.

TODD   There'd be too many, what would they
            do with them?

JOAN   They could reuse them.

TODD   Exactly and then we'd be out of work.

JOAN   It seems so sad to burn them with the
            bodies.

TODD   No I think that's the joy of it. The hats
            are ephemeral. It's like a metaphor for
            something or other.

JOAN   Well, life.

TODD   Well, life, there you are. Out of nearly
            three hundred hats I've made here I've
            only had three win and go in the
            museum. But that's never bothered me.
            You make beauty and it disappears, I
            love that.

JOAN   You're so..

TODD   What?

JOAN   You make me think in different ways.
              Like I'd never have thought about how
              this place is run and now I see how
              important it is.

TODD   I think it did impress a certain person
              that I was speaking from the high
              moral ground.

JOAN   So tell me again exactly what he said at
              the end.

TODD   "These things must be thought about."

JOAN   I think that's encouraging.

TODD   It could mean he'll think how to get rid
              of me.

JOAN   That's a fantastic shape to start from.

TODD   It's a new one for me. I'm getting
              inspired by you.

JOAN   There's still the journalist. If he looks
              into it a bit more we could expose the
              corrupt financial basis of how the whole
              hat industry is run, not just this place,
              I bet the whole industry is dodgy.

TODD   Do you think so?

JOAN   I think we should find out.

TODD   You've changed my life, do you know
            that?

JOAN   If you lose your job I'll resign.

TODD   We might not get jobs in hats again.

JOAN   There's other parades.

TODD   But I think you're a hat genius.

JOAN   Unless all the parades are corrupt.

TODD   I love these beads. Use these beads.

JOAN   No, you have them.

TODD   No, you.

3.

Several years later. HARPER*'s house, daytime.*

HARPER   You were right to poison the wasps.

TODD   Yes, I think all the wasps have got to go.

HARPER   I was outside yesterday on the edge of the wood when a shadow came over and it was a cloud of butterflies, and they came down just beyond me and the trees and bushes were red with them. Two of them clung to my arm, I was terrified, one of them got in my hair, I managed to squash them.

TODD   I haven't had a problem with butterflies.

HARPER   They can cover your face. The Romans used to commit suicide with gold leaf, just flip it down their throat and it covered their windpipe, I think of that with butterflies.

TODD
I was passing an orchard, there were horses standing under the trees, and suddenly wasps attacked them out of the plums. There were the horses galloping by screaming with their heads made of wasp. I wish she'd wake up.

HARPER
We don't know how long she'd been walking.

TODD
She was right to come.

HARPER
You don't go walking off in the middle of a war.

TODD
You do if you're escaping.

HARPER
We don't know that she was escaping.

TODD
She was getting to a place of safety to regroup.

HARPER
Is this a place of safety?

TODD
Relatively, yes of course it is. Everyone thinks it's just a house.

HARPER
The cats have come in on the side of the French.

TODD
I never liked cats, they smell, they scratch, they only like you because you feed them, they bite, I used to have a

cat that would suddenly just take some bit of you in its mouth.

HARPER   Did you know they've been killing babies?

TODD   Where's that?

HARPER   In China. They jump in the cots when nobody's looking.

TODD   But some cats are still ok.

HARPER   I don't think so.

TODD   I know a cat up the road.

HARPER   No, you must be careful of that.

TODD   But we're not exactly on the other side from the French. It's not as if they're the Moroccans and the ants.

HARPER   It's not as if they're the Canadians, the Venezuelans and the mosquitoes.

TODD   It's not as if they're the engineers, the chefs, the children under five, the musicians.

HARPER   The car salesmen.

TODD   Portuguese car salesmen.

HARPER   Russian swimmers.

TODD   Thai butchers.

HARPER   Latvian dentists.

TODD   No, the Latvian dentists have been
            doing good work in Cuba. They've a
            house outside Havana.

HARPER   But Latvia has been sending pigs to
            Sweden. The dentists are linked to
            international dentistry and that's where
            their loyalty lies, with dentists in Dar-
            es-Salaam.

TODD   We don't argue about Dar-es-Salaam.

HARPER   You would attempt to justify the
            massacre in Dar-es-Salaam?

            She's come here because you're here on
            leave and if anyone finds out I'll be
            held responsible.

TODD   It's only till tomorrow. I'll wake her up.
            I'll give her a few more minutes.

HARPER   Did you see the programme about
            crocodiles?

TODD   Yes but crocodiles, the way they look
            after the baby crocodiles and carry

them down to the water in their
mouths.

HARPER   Don't you think everyone helps their
           own children?

TODD   I'm just saying I wouldn't be sorry if
           the crocodiles were on one of the sides
           we have alliances with. They're
           unstoppable, come on.

HARPER   Crocodiles are evil and it is always right
           to be opposed to crocodiles. Their skin,
           their teeth, the foul smell of their
           mouths from the dead meat. Crocodiles
           wait till zebras are crossing the river
           and bite the weak ones with those
           jaws and pull them down. Crocodiles
           invade villages at night and take
           children out of their beds. A crocodile
           will carry a dozen heads back to the
           river, tenderly like it carries its young,
           and put them in the water where they
           bob about as trophies till they rot.

TODD   I'm just saying we could use that.

HARPER   And the fluffy little darling waterbirds,
           the smallest one left behind squeaking
           wait for me, wait for me. And their
           mother who would give her life to save
           them.

TODD   Do we include mallards in this?

HARPER   Mallards are not a good waterbird.
                They commit rape, and they're on the
                side of the elephants and the Koreans.
                But crocodiles are always in the wrong.

TODD   Do you think I should wake her up or
                let her sleep? We won't get any time
                together.

HARPER   You agree with me about the
                crocodiles?

TODD   What's the matter? you don't know
                whose side I'm on?

HARPER   I don't know what you think.

TODD   I think what we all think.

HARPER   Take deer.

TODD   You mean sweet little bambis?

HARPER   You mean that ironically?

TODD   I mean it sarcastically.

HARPER   Because they burst out of parks and
                storm down from mountains and
                terrorise shopping malls. If the does run
                away when you shoot they run into

somebody else and trample them with their vicious little shining hooves, the fawns get under the feet of shoppers and send them crashing down escalators, the young bucks charge the plate glass windows –

TODD   I know to hate deer.

HARPER   and the old ones, do you know how heavy their antlers are or how sharp the prongs are when they twist into teenagers running down the street?

TODD   Yes I do know that.

               He lifts his shirt and shows a scar.

HARPER   Was that a deer?

TODD   In fact it was a bear. I don't like being doubted.

HARPER   It was when the elephants went over to the Dutch, I'd always trusted elephants.

TODD   I've shot cattle and children in Ethiopia. I've gassed mixed troops of Spanish, computer programmers and dogs. I've torn starlings apart with my bare hands. And I liked doing it with my bare hands. So don't suggest I'm not reliable.

HARPER   I'm not saying you can't kill.

TODD   And I know it's not all about
             excitement. I've done boring jobs. I've
             worked in abattoirs stunning pigs and
             musicians and by the end of the day
             your back aches and all you can see
             when you shut your eyes is people
             hanging upside down by their feet.

HARPER   So you'd say the deer are vicious?

TODD   We've been over that.

HARPER   If a hungry deer came into the yard
             you wouldn't feed it?

TODD   Of course not.

HARPER   I don't understand that because the
             deer are with us. They have been for
             three weeks.

TODD   I didn't know. You said yourself.

HARPER   Their natural goodness has come
             through. You can see it in their soft
             brown eyes.

TODD   That's good news.

HARPER   You hate the deer. You admire the
             crocodiles.

TODD   I've lost touch because I'm tired.

HARPER   You must leave.

TODD   I'm your family.

HARPER   Do you think I sleep?

             JOAN *comes in and walks into* TODD*'s*
             arms.

HARPER   You can't stay here, they'll be after you.
             What are you going to say when you
             go back, you ran off to spend a day
             with your husband? Everyone has
             people they love they'd like to see or
             anyway people they'd rather see than
             lie in a hollow waiting to be bitten by
             ants. Are you not going back at all
             because if you're not you might as well
             shoot me now. Did anyone see you
             leave? which way did you come? were
             you followed? There are ospreys here
             who will have seen you arrive. And
             you're risking your life for you don't
             know what because he says things that
             aren't right. Don't you care? Maybe
             you don't know right from wrong
             yourself, what do I know about you
             after two years, I'd like to be glad to
             see you but how can I?

JOAN   Of course birds saw me, everyone saw
me walking along but nobody knew
why, I could have been on a mission,
everyone's moving about and no one
knows why, and in fact I killed two cats
and a child under five so it wasn't that
different from a mission, and I don't
see why I can't have one day and then
go back, I'll go on to the end after this.
It wasn't so much the birds I was
frightened of, it was the weather, the
weather here's on the side of the
Japanese. There were thunderstorms all
through the mountains, I went through
towns I hadn't been before. The rats
are bleeding out of their mouths and
ears, which is good, and so were the
girls by the side of the road. It was
tiring there because everything's been
recruited, there were piles of bodies and
if you stopped to find out there was one
killed by coffee or one killed by pins,
they were killed by heroin, petrol,
chainsaws, hairspray, bleach, foxgloves,
the smell of smoke was where we were
burning the grass that wouldn't serve.
The Bolivians are working with gravity,
that's a secret so as not to spread
alarm. But we're getting further with
noise and there's thousands dead of

light in Madagascar. Who's going to
mobilise darkness and silence? that's
what I wondered in the night. By the
third day I could hardly walk but I got
down to the river. There was a camp of
Chilean soldiers upstream but they
hadn't seen me and fourteen black and
white cows downstream having a drink
so I knew I'd have to go straight across.
But I didn't know whose side the river
was on, it might help me swim or it
might drown me. In the middle the
current was running much faster, the
water was brown, I didn't know if that
meant anything. I stood on the bank a
long time. But I knew it was my only
way of getting here so at last I put one
foot in the river. It was very cold but
so far that was all. When you've just
stepped in you can't tell what's going
to happen. The water laps round your
ankles in any case.